To Smiley —

I do hope you
enjoy reading these
letters —

Yours aye

Ann

LETTERS TO MOLLY

A collection of letters from a nautical father
to his four year old daughter written when he was away
between 1921 and 1924.

Compiled by Ann Thompson

MARIDADI PUBLISHING

First published in 2010 by Maridadi Publishing

2 4 6 8 10 9 7 5 3 1

A CIP catalogue record for this book is available from
The British Library.

ISBN 978-0-9565665-0-8

Cover design by Marcus Thompson

Printed in Great Britain by The MPG Books Group,
Bodmin and King's Lynn

To my sister
Mary Douglas Pawsey
(Molly)
who was wise enough to keep these letters.

Molly read them to her children and grandchildren
and is happy that they may now give pleasure to others.

Acknowledgements

I am grateful to Molly's children,
Susan Barden, Bridget Booth and Roger Pawsey, who
remember their grandfather well. They separately shared
their memories with me and encouraged me to
publish the letters.

My thanks also to Steve Carr, Victoria Whetter, Jim Woolward
and Roger Eaton for their help and encouragement.

FOREWORD

We moderns sometimes think we have invented fatherhood, and that the generations of men who went before were stiff, distant, almost robotic in their manliness. Which is of course, nonsense. Men have always loved their children, and yearned towards them through long absences.

When I first saw these letters, from Arthur Booth to his little daughter Molly, I turned the pages with tearful delight. A waste of oceans divided him for long months from his family, but in his letters the bond was forged and strengthened so that she has kept them all her life, and her sisters have shared the pleasure. Apart from the charming drawings, what is striking is that in every word he wrote this strong, professional seafarer knew exactly how to communicate to a small child. Sitting in his cabin or in some quiet corner of the deck, in heat and cold, surrounded by tough men he yet could share her vision. From the first moments of describing the "twinkling fairy lights" on the Leas as his ship moved out into the great darkness and noticing the Pilot's little white collar as a child would, he describes the oddities of his voyages, and expresses the risks and dangers of his life without alarming her: always conveying warmth, familiarity, the essence of Daddy still with his family though so far away.

Because of the childlike perceptions he enters into, his letters offer us a view of his times too, more vivid and immediate than most nautical histories. But above all, they show us what it is to be a loving father, out in the world earning a living amid adult complications and stresses, yet able to turn to his child with the same innocent wonder that she herself would have. It is a portrait of mutual refreshment, and of family, and as such a precious document for us all.

Libby Purves

June 2010

CONTENTS

INTRODUCTION

INTRODUCTION

Arthur John Booth DSC
Master Mariner
1891 - 1980

Arthur Booth was born in Aylesbury, Buckinghamshire and grew up in Streatham Hill, London. While he was at Dulwich College in 1908, his father arranged an indentured apprenticeship in the four-masted barque *Nile* owned by Boyd & Co. of Glasgow, which traded to Australia, the west coast of the USA, Chile and Japan with several trips around Cape Horn.

In 1912 he transferred from sail to steam and served on *SS Volumnia*, *Tiverton* and *Oakdale* during which time he studied for his Second and First Mate tickets. When the war broke out in 1914, he was Second Mate on *SS Brighton*, which was painted as a hospital ship and went across the Channel collecting wounded soldiers. In 1915 he studied for his Certificate of Competency and qualified as Master of a foreign-going ship. He then joined *RMS Ulster* and volunteered for Naval Service in Dublin joining the Royal Naval Reserve initially as a Sub-Lieutenant on 31st October 1915.

His war service from 1915 to 1919 was varied - the Royal Navy "knocked him into shape" and, after the initial training with *HMS Excellent* at Portsmouth, he was sent as Boarding Officer to *HMT Tenby Castle,* part of the 10th Cruiser Squadron operating south of Iceland, preventing neutral ships from running the blockade to Germany.

He was serving on *HMS Victory* in 1917 when he had leave and married Mary Miller in Yorkshire.

On his return to duty he was sent to *HMS Stonecrop* (launched as *Glenfoyle*), which was being converted as a "Q" ship under Commander M Blackwood DSO, RN. It looked like a harmless tramp steamer but had hidden guns and a crew of 99. Arthur Booth was in charge of the 'panic party', which would abandon ship when challenged by a submarine on the surface. Hopefully the submarine would sail nearer the abandoned ship to know the ship's name and possibly steal victuals. It was then that the RN crew hidden aboard would open fire and attempt to sink the submarine.

It was on 17th September 1917, that a submarine believed to be the infamous *U88* took *Stonecrop* to be a harmless trader and surfaced approaching the ship. The 'panic party' took to the two lifeboats and the submarine became more confident and sailed closer. The men still hidden aboard awaited the command to 'let go'. The flaps went down with a crash and the previously concealed guns opened fire.

There followed an exchange of gunfire after which the submarine's nose came up and her stern went down until she was lying at an angle of 45 degrees. Despite attempts by the crew to right their vessel, she sank stern first. Fifteen seconds later she again rose to the surface, with her conning tower just out of the water, but with a heavy list to starboard. A few seconds later she finally disappeared beneath the surface.

Unfortunately, only 24 hours afterwards a torpedo hit *Stonecrop*, which sank rapidly and only two lifeboats and a raft survived. Arthur Booth's lifeboat travelled some 120 miles in very cold and rough conditions and after 3 days landed in Bantry Bay, Southern Ireland. Commander Blackwood's lifeboat was sighted by a warship and the crew were taken aboard. The raft, however, spent over 6 days drifting, and of the 3 officers and 20 men aboard, only 2 officers and 8 men survived the terrible days of hunger, thirst and exposure. Of *Stonecrop's* total complement of 99, 4 officers and 40 men had lost their lives.

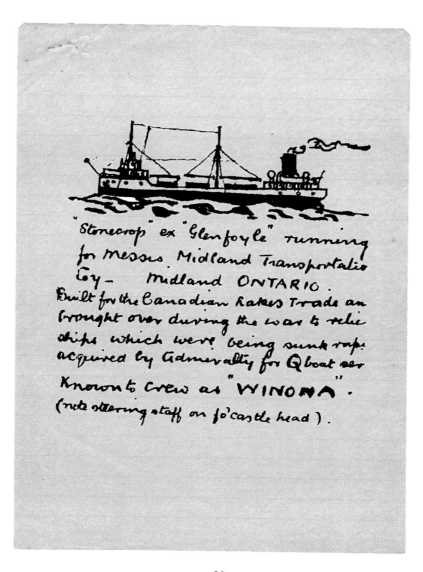

"Stonecrop" ex "Glenfoyle" running for messrs. Midland Transportatio Coy – Midland ONTARIO. Built for the Canadian lakes trade an brought over during the war to relie ships which were being sunk rap: acquired by Admiralty for Q boat ser Known to crew as "WINONA". (note steering staff on fo'castle head).

Arthur Booth's eldest daughter Molly was born in March 1918 and he was demobilised on 6 February 1919 joining *RRS Discovery* as First Mate. He then went to *SS Menominee* until he accepted a job as Marine Officer with the South Eastern & Chatham Railway, living with his family in Folkestone and serving on the cross Channel steamers to France. In August 1920 his second daughter, Elizabeth, was born.

AJB

Officers of South Eastern & Chatham Railway 1920

In 1921, after two years, Arthur Booth answered an advertisement seeking an Assistant Wharf Master in Tampico, Mexico. He sailed on the Eagle Oil tanker *SS San Patricio* and began writing his monthly letters to his four year old daughter.

S.S. San "Patricio"
Out ward bound.
June 1921.

My dear Molly

Mother has returned home after
seeing me go away in a big ship
from Gravesend, and I do hope you
are looking after her, and also Baby
Elizabeth, for we shall all be very
lonely for some time
The ship will very soon pass
Folkestone and our little house, but
you will be in byes and all I
will see will be nothing but a few
twinkling fairy lights which mark
The Leas where you play. Then the
ship will haul out on her course
to the "Ness".
I shall give this letter to The Pilot
who is such a nice man with a
jolly face and little white collar
and the smallest of black bows.

1

Now you will know when you see
a pilot next time!
I like Pilots don't you?
They make you feel safe somehow,
for they know such a lot about
rivers and winding in and out
channels. But they only learn
to take a ship one way that's so
they won't get mixed up and think
they are coming home when they
are going outwards.
Our Pilot has just taken us past
the Goodwin Sands which they say
once was part of a gentleman's
garden, long long ago.
It's a very dangerous corner for
sailormen, and they have to be
dreadfully dreadfully careful.
Mr Pilotman is ready to go down
the Jacob's ladder into his little
boat as we are near Dover.
        I must hurry up and finish
this else I'll miss him and then

2

you wouldn't get a letter for ever so long, weeks and weeks perhaps. It's awfully difficult for the pilot to get down the ladder in rough weather for one minute his little boat is high up on a wave then deep down.

I think it was a good job for the Angels that the ladder Jacob dreamed about did not get twisted like the pilot's else the angels would never have climbed down, but they might, for they had wings to help them which the pilot hasn't, if he ever had I 'spict he left them at the "Flying Angel mission" when he was a little boy.

Between ourselves Molly, I'm not so sure as Dick Whittington was that I'll make heaps & heaps of money in Mexico

3

I can't make Bow Bells ring promises
for me, and although they say if
you listen very carefully to chiming
bells they will tell you what you
would like to hear. That may be so
but the bell on the buoy we have
just passed is ringing a very sad
tune like

" Ding Dong Bell Pussy's in the well"
and no matter how hard I try,
or on which side of the ship I
listen I cannot make it say to
me.

" Turn again Whittington Lord Mayor
    of London".

Kiss Baby Elizabeth for me and
write & tell me how tall the
hollyhock's grown. It's racing
you I think. Have the flowers I
planted in the old dust bin come
to any thing? I liked that old
garden of ours & still can see in
my little mind's eye

Baby Elizabeth using a big sunflower leaf for an umbrella.

My love to mother & you all

Ever Your Daddy.

P.S.

All the names I know from Nurse
Gardeners Garters, Shepherds purse
Bachelors buttons, Lady's smock
And the LADY HOLLYHOCK.

Fair are grown up peoples trees
But the fairest woods are these
Where if I were not so tall
I should live for good and all

R.L.S.

MOLLY AND
THE
HOLLYHOCK.

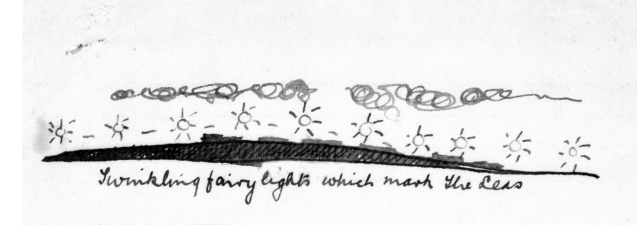

Twinkling fairy lights which mark the Leas

SHIPS THAT TOOK THE WRONG TURNING

WAVES BANGING
AND SPRAY
WHICH TASTES SALTY

SOUTH GOODWIN

THE GOODWIN SANDS

HIS BAG,

SWAK

YOUR LETTER
IN HIS
BAG

DING — DONG.

Tampico Bay.
July 1921.

My dear Molly..
        I have just arrived in
Mexico which they call "The Land
Of Beautiful Sunsets".

The ship stole in quietly to night
as if feeling its way as one does
in the dark when going up stairs
to bed.
The Captain dropped his Anchor
with a loud splash deep down
among the oysters and coral
then all was very still and silent
Oh such a big silence after so
long of listening to the throb of the
engines and the swish swash of
the waves. The soughing of the wind

has sung us to sleep for the last
three weeks and we miss him.
Then all of a sudden we heard a
train whistle from out of the long
black line which the Captain tells
me is the shore.

Close by is the sound of a honk!
honk! of a big goose returning to
her home in the marshes.

So we really know at last that
we are in Mexico, for every now
and again a big white light
winks at us and then goes out.

The sailormen have pulled
down the coloured pretty lights
they show at night and all gone
to bed very tired except a very
old gentleman, an old man of the
sea, very very old with grey hair
who was "borned" as you say long
before you were.

He is sitting in the galley

smoking a black clay pipe with a
tin cover over it

He is looking after the ship I think.
He tells me that the cook
has not left him much of a BLACK
PAN which I think means his
supper.
But I don't think he has been
naughty as little girls sometimes
are who have to go to bed without
any, but that the COOK has just
forgotten.

- Mr Sun

Next day.

When MR Sun rose big and red
in the East where you are from me
the Captain hove up his anchor
which funny sailormen call a
"pick"

I don't know why.
and we went alongside the pier.
Then we all got out except the
sailors who just went on with
their work as if nothing had
happened at all.

There seems a lot of men here
besides your Daddy coming out
to get bread and butty money
for their little girls, but there does
not seem to be many houses
for us to stay in although

carpenters are busy making some
more; they use very sharp tools
but do not cut their fingers

I was very glad to get ashore
and see the coco nuts waving
in the wind on the end of a long
stem and a little tuft on top

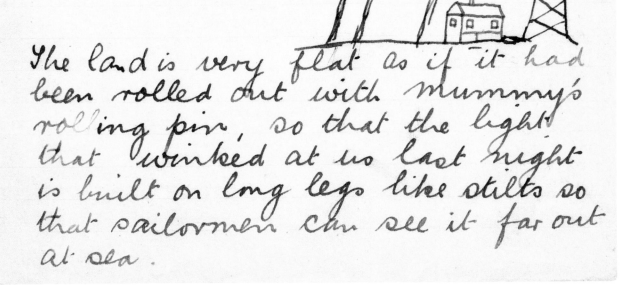

The land is very flat as if it had
been rolled out with mummy's
rolling pin, so that the light
that winked at us last night
is built on long legs like stilts so
that sailormen can see it far out
at sea.

I've got such a funny house to stay in, its near the light house, coco nut trees and the sea.side. Its what the estate man down your road would call " a desirable sea.side residence". (no bath, no H & C). Another man is living with me called Mac, he is very clever and makes engines, not puffing billies and big steam rollers that blow out steam like mummy's kettle but 'lectric. ones that go without any noise He is not a bit afraid of lightning or thunder and he tells me he can harness lightning just like you can a horsey and make it do lots and lots for him. He is ever so clever but hasn't any little girls like you and Elizabeth so he is quite pleased to hear about you.

12

The mosquitoes are humming
very loud like the aeroplanes
that fly so high over Folkestone
also I see thousands of twinkling
lights that come and go which
they say are fire flies

MAN WITH RED FLAG.

ALL THEIR OWN WORK

ROAD UP

HMS FURY   K.C.o

Big steam Rollers.

No more news I'll write again
soon   best love to you all
Ever your loving
Daddy.

Tampico
August 1921

My dear Molly
        I was very glad to get mother's
letter for it seems a long time since
I had news of you.
I was very sorry to hear that you had
been very poorly and the Doctor had
been worried about you so much
that you had to take lots of nasty
medicine.
It was a fine game you were having
with the doctor man.
He thought you had been out in the
hot sun too much and after you
had been very ill and Mummy
very very anxious with a big
frown on her forehead with watching
you tell them all you had eaten
some "little peas" you had found
in the garden.   It was a good
thing you didn't share them

15

with Baby sister Elizabeth; but I
think even she would not have
eaten them.
Those "little peas" were laburnum
seeds from the "golden chain" tree
and very bad for little girls
You ought never to taste even a
little nibble of anything you find
for some plants and flowers,
although they are very pretty give
little girls and little boys too heaps
and heaps of stomach-ache
which usually means BED
lots of CASTOR OIL and no cakes.
Kiss mother and Baby Elizabeth
for me and tell her I am glad
you are better.
Don't eat "little peas" again though.

Ever your loving
Daddy!

Tampico
September 1921.

My dear Molly.

Mother tells me that you can now make beautiful ◯ s and ✕ s with your pencil.

I expect you will soon be able to draw pictures of ducks and bunnies like this .

I am very fond of drawing aren't you? especially on rainy days when the rain is beating down outside and we cannot go shopping with Mother.

I've drawn a little picture of a house when it's raining very hard outside; I think all the little children are inside playing, and their mother is very busy sewing and mending such big holes in their Daddy's socks; he wears out such a lot of socks you see because he is a post-man and has such a long way to walk every morning dropping letters in the letter box and banging the door Rat-tat! Rat tat!

Mother tells me Elizabeth can walk around a chair now like this

This is not a very good picture.

Don't it clever of her 'cos she is such a little mite?

There's Beth with a balloon in her hand.

At La Barra where I live two big pigs have such a lot of little ones, they go grunting around digging up roots with their little noses: they do not go very far from their mother piggie though.

There is too a dear little baby Neddy and some little white kids their mother and father are named Nanny and Billy goat.
Nanny is very nice and quiet, but Billy has a funny little beard and horns
He has horns so he can look after his family and fight any one who tries to hurt them.

I do not think I have any more
to tell you just now molly.
I hope you are good to Mother
whom Daddy loves and that
you are being a little mother
yourself to Beth.
I hope too, if you are in the street
and have some sweeties you will
not forget to give some to a little
boy or girlie whom you meet
who might be cold and not
have any pennies to buy any
with.
Love and kisses from Daddy
and put your arms right round
mother's neck and give her a big
kiss and then do the same to
Liz.

Ever your own
Daddy.

Tampico
October 1921

My dear Molly

Just a little letter to thank
you very much for the one
you wrote to Daddy a little
while ago.
I hope you and little Beth
are having a good time and
that specially you are taking
care of mother and helping her
to be happy while I am away.
Such a funny thing happened
to day as I lay in bed (for I
had been working making big
ships very fast so that the wind
would not blow
them away all the night long)
such a pretty little bird flew
into my bed room.
He cocked his little head on one
side as if to say.
"Good morning mr man how do
you do"!

21

He made himself quite at home
and flew up into the rafters.
and ate such a lot of flies.
I was glad he did for they tickle
my nose very much.
After he had become tired of
chasing flies he perched on a
clothes line that I tied across
the room to dry my clothes on.
Mother would say quite a lot to
me I expect if she was here for
it is not very tidy of me is it?
I know you don't hang clothes
in your bed-room but properly
in the kitchen.

Last night I went up the
river in a little boat and as
we sailed quietly (not making
a sound) round a bend
we saw an old stork with long
legs and a big beak standing on
the edge of the river paddling.
He was not a bit frightened and

went on with his fishing
and looked very wise
like this

my love to all.
Ever your own
Daddy

The friendly
Miss Blots.

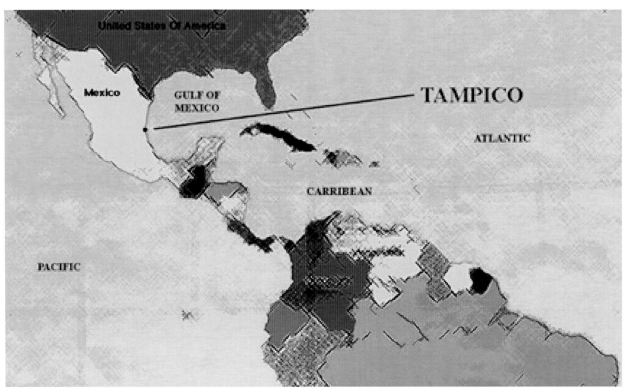

Tampico
November 1921.

My dear Molly,
    I saw this pretty picture of a
garden and I thought you would like
to see it too as it has pretty colours.
I think the flowers must be wall
flowers although I am not quite sure.
I wonder if I can make up a little
bit of poetry about gilly flowers I'll
try so here goes.

"Little wall-flower growing on the garden wall
"Tell me why you bloom there at all"
"Surely in all the garden fair".
"a Better spot you'd find".
To let your fragrance fall on all around"

There's three more verses of this but I
think one is PLENTY, and we can
leave it unfinished I say
"More next week".

25

The flowers in Mexico are bigger than those where you live molly but Daddy does not think they smell as sweet as those that you and I planted in Folkestone in Mother's little garden.

I hope you are liking staying at Grandmas.

I used to like staying with her very much you get lovely "sleepy-byes" in her big four poster beds.

I used to lie awake sometimes and listen very hard. And then if it is very quiet at night you can hear the water in the river rippling over the stones. You listen too, and then ask mother nicely if she can make what the river is saying on the piano. I think mother can do it for you, then you can really hear what the River says to the waterfall.

Daddy calls it the River's Singing Voice

Give my love to Mother and kiss
her for me and also give my love
to little Elizabeth who I hope you
look after & help such a lot and
take care of your big Mummy

Ever your Daddy.

Tampico
November 1921.

My dear Molly.

Good morning, how are you
old thing And how is little Elizabeth
and mother?

I am very well.

I thought I would write to you to tell
you that last night just as the sun
was setting very many geese and
ducks came flying over here from
the North.

There were hundreds of them and they
flew like this with big black
ganders leading; the rest of them
had white feathers.

29

I'll tell you how they came here.

They really live in little nests built among the reeds and rushes that grow round the lakes in Canada. They have enjoyed the warm summer very much, flying from lake to lake and splashing and paddling about looking for frogs in the ponds and streams.

Frogs take a lot of catching because they can swim very fast and dive too just like Mother Can.

Well these old ducks and geese waited around until one morning they woke up & found they were cold and all had stiff necks. They thought at first it was with sleeping standing on one leg that had given them cramp so the first night they did not mind, but next night the cold wind blew from off the ice and ruffled up their feathers so they huddled together and snuggled up to keep.

themselves warm until the morning.
When they woke up all the old birds
said to the young ones
"It's time to go to Mexico where it is
warm".
So the young birds thought it was
such a good idea, that they said
they would go if the old Father
and mother birds would show them
the way.
The old ducks had often been to
Mexico, so they knew all they had
to do was to follow the rivers and
streams and look out for big
mountains, waterfalls, and lakes
which their own Fathers and mothers
had told them about before.
They knew all the names of the
places they came to on the way.
They called one "Big mountain", & a
big pond. "Crystal Lake" because
it was deep clear & blue.
They called the river they followed

"Snake River" because it wound in and out in a long wriggley line

well they started off amid such a lot of quacking, the big old wise father ducks went first then all the little quackers.

The old ducks said to the young ones "Keep a good look-out for "Big Mountain" and the wriggly River so next year you come again you will be able to find your way and not get lost. Who do you think saw them off on their long journey? A little kit fox! He said he was very sorry to lose them but he thought they ought to go. Then what do you think he did? He changed his fur coat. He had a brown fur coat for the summer, not too heavy Molly, but just a nice weight, but when he saw the quackers go away he put on a heavy white fur coat.

He was really a very wise kit foe
for his age for he said to himself
my white coat will keep me warm,
and in the snow which is white no
one will see me & try to catch me. 'cos
now I'm white too and he laughed
to himself a deep Wow-oo- Wow-oo.
    By this time the ducks had got
a long way; they had passed by
The Lake of the Woods, the Big Mountain,
The Snake River and were still a
long way from Mexico. About
half way I think. The little ducks
wanted to rest but the big old
ducks said "No! let's hurry on".
So that's where they were going Molly
when they flew over my head
last evening. They had only a few
more miles to go which made them
very happy for they knew that
they would find cosy places to
rest down by the side of the
Lagoon.

I'm glad they have found their
way here all right.
Now they will be quite comfy
until Spring time when the trees
begin to grow again, and the little
kit fox changes into his brown
coat & calls.
"Ducks and Quackers; it's time you
all came back to Canada, everything
smells good round here, the
snow is gone away and the
sleepy ground hog is about and
there are some beautiful places
where you can build your nests
and lay bluey green eggs.
So when Spring time comes the
quackers will remember the way
they have come and hurry back
again.

    I wish I could fly home
like the ducks I wouldn't stop
like the little ducks wanted to do
but hurry on.

Kiss mother & Beth for me.
Cheerio oh molly oh!
Daddy.

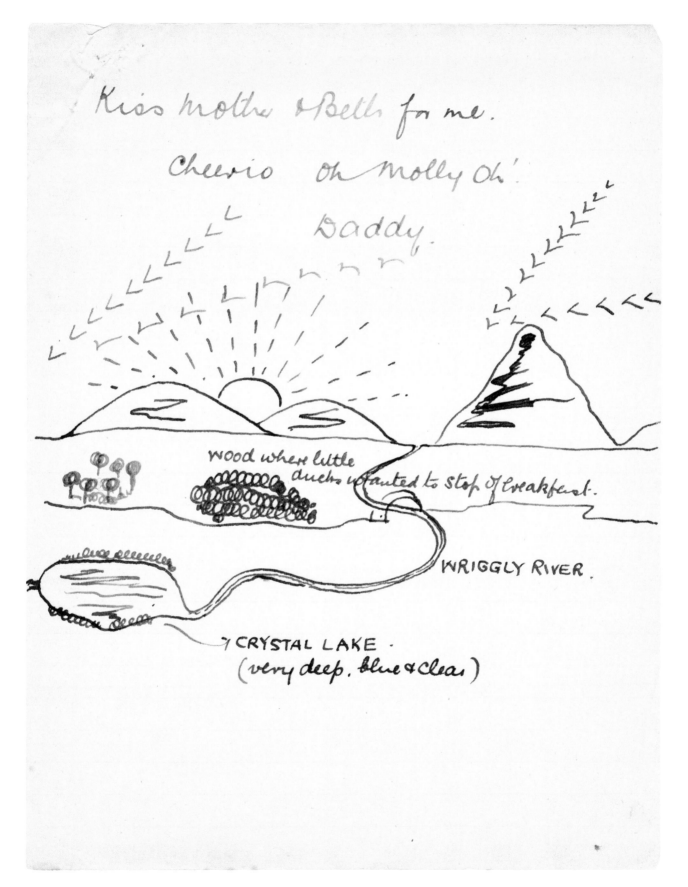

wood where little
ducks wanted to stop of breakfast.

WRIGGLY RIVER.

CRYSTAL LAKE.
(very deep, blue & clear)

Tampico
December 1921.

My dear Molly.
    I hope mother, Elizabeth and
you have spent a very happy
Christmas
I was working myself, but all the
little children had a party on
Christmas afternoon.
They had a Christmas tree too, but
it had to be brought such a long
way from the woods in the cold
northland that the heat of mexico
made it droop very much & even
water did not revive it much.
    Daddy feels like that a bit;
and would like to get to a cold
country and live once again
in a little house with mother
Elizabeth & you.
Wouldn't that be fine?

A friend of mine who lives next
door went to a party for grown up
folks and it was not over until 3 o'clock
in the morning.
Nearly everybody was fast asleep by
then.
Coming back from the party he met
an old donkey so he jumped on
his back and rode down to the
factory gates.
He came through the yard gate with
his arms round the old donkey's
neck and what do you think the
watchman said to him?
"The pass is all right for yourself
Senōr but what about the donkey?"
My friend was very tired and sleepy
so he told the watchman he would
write out a pass for Neddy too.
So he sat down & wrote
"Please pass Senōr Hee Haw
through the main Depot Gate."
Wasn't that funny?

The old donkey was amused.
I saw this pretty little picture[*]
to day and I thought that one rainy
day you could paint it.
I think the little girl would look
well in a blue dress don't you?
Kiss mummy and Beth for me

Ever your Daddy.

* Unfortunately lost over time

39

Tampico
January 1922

My dear Molly,

I haven't had a letter from you for a long time although I have had heaps and heaps from Mother.

She tells me you have been riding about in such a lot of trains lately I wish I could have come with you.

How did you enjoy yourself with your cousins in Edinburgh? I hope you were pally and jolly with them.

I expect all the shop windows were made ever so pretty with toys and dolls.

Did you see any Christmas trees, and Old Santa Claus in a Red Cloak? I do like Yule time & so does Mother.

I read such a "sleepy byes" song.

41

that you can learn & sing to Liz.
It is the song that black Mammies
sing to their little black babies.

" Sleep my little pigeon don't you hear
                    your mammy coo?"
" Sunset still a shining in the West."
" Sky am full of windows, and the stars
                    are peeping thro'".
" Everything but mammy's lamb at rest.

    " Swing him to the Eastland"
      " Swing him to the South".
  " See that dove acoming with an olive in
                        his mouth".
  " Angel harps, a humming".
  " Angel banjos strumming"
  " Sleep my little pigeon don't you hear
                    your mammy coo."

"Cricket fiddler scraping the resin from his
                                                        bow"
"Whipp o' will a moaning on a log"
"moon as pale as it can be,
                rising mighty slow."
"Startled at the barking of a dog".

" Swing the baby Eastway"
    " Swing the baby West."
" Swing him to the South-land
            "Where the melons grow the best.
    "Angel singers singing"
    " Angel bells a ringing"
    " Sleep my little pigeon don't you hear your
                                    mammy coo."

    "
      Eyelids just a drooping little lover all
                                    the while"
    " Underlip a sagging just a mite "
    " Little baby toothies, showing sort o' like a
                                    smile "
        "
          Whiter than the snow or just as white"

43

Swing him to the Northland"
"Swing him to the East."
"Wooly cloud a-coming to wrap'
         him in its fleece."
"Angel band a playing"
    "What's that music saying?"
"Sleep my little pigeon don't you
         hear your mammy coo".

Strickland W. Gillilan
from "Including
   Finnigin".

All my love
    from Daddy.

Tampico
February. 1922.

My dear Molly.

I have cut this picture* out of a picture book and as I haven't very much to talk about I thought we would write about it.

I know you will like the little girl in the picture, she is such a friendly happy little girl just about as big as you.

The boat in the picture belongs to her Daddy who is a fisherman and all through the summer when the weather was fine he used to go out into the sea in his little boat to catch fishes.

He used to go at night because the fishes could not see the net in the dark and got caught better.

* Unfortunately lost over time

45

now it is windy, cold and stormy
on the sea he has hauled his little
boat up on the beach which the
fisherman calls "the hard".

He has now come ashore to live
with his little girl and her mummy
until Spring time comes again.
You will wonder where he will
get pennies to buy bread and
butter with now that he does not
go out catching fishes.
Well during the summer he saved
up all his pennies & put them in
a little tin box; so now he can
go to the grocery man and the butcher
and buy food for them all with
the pennies he takes one by one from
the money box.
You know all those big Bumble
Bees that go from flower to flower
going right inside of the "bunny
mouths" of the Snap dragons!
weren't they busy gathering honey?

They work so hard in the summer
too and carry it back to their
hives for they too know that
when the cold weather comes, there
will be no flowers and they
may die too
So they gather honey while they may
just as the fisherman catches silver
fishes while he can.

That's Daddy's story.
Kisses & Love to you and Elizabeth

Daddy.

Tampico
March 1922.

My dear Molly and Elizabeth.

I am counting the days now when you and Mother will arrive in the big ship from England.

I have every thing ready for you, a little house quite different to the one in Folkestone, all made of wood and what do you think? You do not go up stairs for bed, but just through a door into another room.

Round the house is a veranda where you can both play. It is propped up on big legs which stand in nasty oil to keep the creepy crawlies from climbing up into the house.
You have a nice nursery, and to make it pretty Mr Mac and I have cut out pictures out of big ladies' magazines and pasted them on the wall.

Its just like an Underground
Station in London where Grandma
lives. Won't that be nice?
You will be able to lie in bed half
asleep & look at the pictures on the wall
and tell Liz about them.
There are two little white beds in
the room and you two little girls will
have to go to bye byes under a big
net like a tent as soldiers do.
Then when the mosquitoes come
buzzing around looking for little
girls to bite they won't be able to
get at you & go away disappointed
to try & bite the little girl next door.

There is ever so such a high
swing in the garden and my
friend Bab who tells me "his
Father is buying up a chain
of banks" has made a sundial
for you.
On it he has painted in black
letters.

"
YE GOLDEN HOURS THEY FLY AWAY."
You will be able to tell the time
by it even though mother's tick
tock has stopped.
It throws shadows that's why!
Shadows are funny aren't they
as they flit to and fro.

"The funniest thing about him is
                              the way he likes to
                                                grows"
"
Not at all like proper children which
                is always very slow!"
" For he sometimes shoots up taller   "
                like an india rubber ball"
" And he sometimes gets so little that   "
                there's none of him at all."
                                                R.L.S.
Now molly when you are in the
big boat I want you to be very
very good and look after mummy
and Elyabeth. and specially to
see that Beth who is such a little
mite does not climb out between
the rails & fall into the deep sea.

51

Also another thing.

In the afternoon I want you
to be quite quiet like two little mice
because the sailormen who keep
watch at night want to go to sleep
and get a little nap when they can,
They want plenty of sleep to keep
a good watch looking out for
ships and stars and islands and
all the things that sailors do.

Sailormen sometimes love to
tease little girls, but don't believe
them when they tell you about
the old knotty crocodiles that wink
their watery eyes.
Crocodiles don't like little girls inside
of them as they are tough & give them
pains in the tummy.

Crocodiles only live in rivers on
Cockatoo islands and you are both
coming to Tampico.

So when they try to tease you
just get Mummy's scissors & say
"Crocodile tumming Mr man"
opening & closing the scissors the while
like a "crock" does his jaws.
Then they won't tell you any more
nasty stories about them

    All my love until I
really see you.

      Eve your Daddy.

FAMILY SAIL TO TAMPICO

When a house became available in Tampico in the Spring of 1922, Arthur Booth's wife, Mary, with Molly (aged four) and Elizabeth (aged eighteen months), sailed from England to Mexico on the Eagle Oil Tanker *SS San Ricardo*. It was not unusual for the tankers to be used in this way for employees' families. Mary Booth wrote that '*SS San Ricardo* was in Hull docks and standing very high out of the water - she was end-on to the quay and a great long ladder up over her stern - kindly sailors carried the children up the ladder and when they were all safely aboard, there was no return!'

SS San Ricardo sailed the following day and went down the North Sea in a snowstorm although it was March. It was a very stormy passage and the family all suffered sea-sickness, but gradually they got their sea legs. There was no space for play on the rusty iron decks of the old tankers, and the Steward gave Mary Booth some 6 yards of rope to tie the young child to the rail in the alleyway so that she could run up and down and not go overboard. No further land was sighted for 24 days until the ship arrived in Havana, Cuba, after which they had a pleasant 4-day run to Tampico.

The family were reunited and went to their bungalow at La Barra under the lighthouse with a frontage of sandy beach and palm trees. Mary Booth made a home with the free issue of furniture and the children played happily around the verandah. If they went to bathe in the sea, they took a tin of paraffin and a cloth to clean off the black oil, which was mixed with the sea waves of Miramar.

Booth family home, Tampico, Mexico - 1922

Arthur and Mary Booth with Molly and sister Elizabeth, Tampico 1922

Tampico Wharf 1923

FAMILY LEAVE TAMPICO FOR ENGLAND

Arthur Booth's two year contract with The Mexican Eagle Petroleum Co., "El Aguila", was due to end in July 1923. In April 1923 Molly with her mother and sister sailed from Tampico aboard the tanker *SS San Ugon*, which was loaded with paraffin. It was much newer and more comfortable than the old *Ricardo*, and meals were served with the officers. After a smooth voyage they sailed into Portishead and travelled onwards by train to the grandparents in Yorkshire.

Arthur Booth continued to work in Tampico living a lonely bachelor life but once more wrote monthly letters, now to Molly and Elizabeth.

Tampico
April 1923.

my dear Molly & Elizabeth

It seems such a long time
since you two little girls and
mother sailed away for England
in the big ship.

I stood quite a long time on
the end of the wharf after you had
gone and watched your steamer's
stern light out of sight until I
could not tell it from one of the
low down stars.

Everything in the Colony is
going on just the same. Maria
tells me that since you and mother
have left that "very sad is the
house".

Your swing is just empty and
swaying in the wind.
Swings are meant to be used
by little girls aren't they?

So that they can swing
     "up in the air & over the wall"
          "Till I can see so wide"
     "Rivers and trees and cattle and all"
          "over the country side".
                                    R.L.S.

You know the old pram that was
in the garden? Why all the
climby vines have grown up it
and almost covered it; so soon
do flowers forget.
Mrs Dodds says it makes her
feel quite sad to see it for it
reminds her of "Ponkele" that's
Elizabeth.

The valadoves still blow their
whistles, and creep back into
their watchman's box at night
and snuggle behind their blankets.
The little lame old caretaker next-
door asks about you both and
when you are coming back?

60

I tell him you are having a holiday in Inglaterra and that I hope you will come back "pronto" that's right away, but he does not believe me for so many go away and don't come back any more from their "holidays". Señor Wilson's man still carries the dinners on a pole, and John the Chinaman brings the bread but he leaves no more "make weight cakes" now for the niñas, nor does he ask "if the Señora would like a nice pescado"

It is not quite the same without you all, but I hope I shall see you all soon for I miss you dreadfully.

Look after mother for me.

Ever your loving
Daddy.

Señor Wilsons
Pet Peon.
with dinners
on a pole.

So Soon Do Flowers
Forget.

Tampico.
April 1923

my dear Molly and Elizabeth.

This is just a little line from
Daddy who is wondering how you
are both getting along these bright
Spring days.

I got Mummy's cablegram
which was sent to the "San Tiburcio"
and was very glad to hear that
the sea was not rough on the voyage.
The "San Ugon" did go home quickly;
they must have had good engineers
on board who drove the engines
fast Chunk! Chunk! Chunk! Chunk!
Did you notice how tired the engines
sounded when you were nearly
at the port?
They seemed to say,
"Oh Yes we're tired"
        Oh Yes we're tired."
I suppose there were so many
interesting things to see when you

got home that you would be very excited.

I hope you did not forget to buy mummy a bunch of violets from the first flower lady you saw! But perhaps you would not have any English pennies or would be busy getting all your luggage on the train.

Vera and her mother went home in a ship two days ago. Sonny and Chico are quite lonely now, you see Burny is so busy in the garden planting tulipans that he does not see much of Sonny.

Our rose tree is all in bloom you see Elizabeth has not been able to pick the buds.

The pigeons are making nests too and I see some young ones flying around.

The mother birds that are still sitting on their eggs are doing a lot of cooing

The Daddy birds are away looking for worms and tastey tit bits most of the day but come back at night.

I always think that is a good advertisement

"Fathers if its Nestles
        Come home with the milk"

Give mummy a kiss for me and heaps to your own two selves.

X X X X X X X X X X X X }12 Each.
X X X X X X X X X X X X

[X]

mummy's

Ever your Daddy.

P. S.

It has rained very hard for days
and days.   I fell up to my
neck into a ditch full of water as
I couldn't see the path
and Señor Wilson had to put
all his clothes on top of the
ward-robe.
However you could bring boats
up to the door, but a beautiful
rainbow has come in the sky
so we know it's all right.

Shlosh.

Shlosh

Daddy in
the ditch

centre
of
gravity

Tampico
May 1923.

My dear Molly and Elizabeth.

I hope you are both well and enjoying the summer in England.

I expect there will be heaps of flowers to pick and many more buttercups and daisies than here. When the "Señora" who does my washing (also Señor Wilson's) came yesterday she found a pussy with four little kittens in a kerosene case in the scullery. The mother was that stray black and white pussy that used occasionally to come to see us.

Her little kittens were tabbies. The mother looked hungry so I gave her some bread and milk which she ate up very quickly as she had not had a drink of milk for a long time, but had been catching and eating little field mice out of the garden.

I left them all very comfortable last night, but when I went to give her milk this morning I found the box empty.

I don't know who could have taken them, but I think the ice-man.

I told the mother pussy how very sorry I was she had lost her kittens, and she went mewing away to look round the colony for them. I expect she would find them as they would not be very far away.

Five cats though would have been rather much for the house don't you think?

Since you and Elizabeth left there are a lot more pigeons living in the holes in the roof.

They are coloured white & grey and seem very happy teaching their young ones to fly.

I saw some dear little birdies to day with yellow breasts. They had built a nest under Mr Dodd's veranda which was made of mud and grass. The little ones had long necks with no feathers on. They had their heads out of the nest eager and hungry for the flies that the Father bird was catching for them.

When I passed along to my dinner to day all the little Haro boys & girls were playing in the garden. They all had a ribbon tied round their hair and each had two pigeon feathers stuck up like you see in pictures. They were playing at Wild Indians; long long ago their fathers were perhaps Aztecs

I hope you are enjoying yourselves
and are very good chums, helping
mummy all you can.
I wish I could play wild Indians
with you both, but I hope to be
home with you soon.

All my love
from Daddy.

P.S.   Is the black-bird in the copper
beech this year.

END OF Mexican
ADVENTURES.

GOOD BYE TO THE
CACTUS.

Arthur Booth arrived in England early in August 1923 in time to be home in Yorkshire when his third daughter, Ann, was born. Soon after, he was employed on small coasters off the Irish Free State and once more wrote letters to his children. He then joined *SS Minnie De Larrinaga* transporting cotton from the Southern States of America bound for the cotton mills of Lancashire.

His next job was with the Port of London Authority engaged in dredging the River Thames and deepening the channel from the Nore to Woolwich Reach. This allowed him to have a Monday to Friday job and the family settled in a Victorian house in Blackheath. The hoppers were moored on Friday nights or Saturday mornings and so he was able to enjoy weekends at home with his wife and three daughters.

Eastham Locks.
August 1923.

My dear Molly and Elizabeth.
So this is old England again!
I have rung up Mummy on
the telephone (not Silly!)
and was very glad to hear your
voices again.
I couldn't however get anymore
than a little grunt from Liz
but she never did say much
did she?
I hope to get up to Manchester
tomorrow so I will be home
with you all tomorrow night.
The pilot-man has put the ship
in a lay-by for the night as he
says "there's lots of ships coming down
the Canal and all in a hurry
to get out". Ships always seem
to be in a hurry and go about
puffing and blowing and

73

bumping on.

Tug boats seem to be the fussiest
and busiest of all.

The canal isn't very wide that's
why we have to wait, for it
would never do for two ships
to bump into each other and block
up the canal.

I don't know what the folks up
manchester way would do then.
for they would get no cotton, no
bread and butties and no much bananas.

manchester is a very big city
with lots and lots of houses and
factories, but it is a long way
from the sea. side and up on
top of a big hill.

A long time ago this worried the
people who lived there for they
wanted to bring ships right
up to their factories.

They collected ever so many
pennies in a hat, thousands

thousands and asked clever
engineers to make them a river
from the sea so that ships could
get up.

They started digging this big
hole one very rainy day a long
time ago.
Daddy's grandpa & grandma
were there and lots of other people.
The engineers had a lot of trouble to
keep the water in as Manchester
was high up and the sea was
deep down so they made big
gates here and there to keep the
water in.
The sailormen call these locks,
so when a boat has to go up to
Manchester it is like having
to go up a lot of steps like this

SHIPS GOING UP STEPS.

The pilot man has told the captain
to lower down his masts else
we might knock the puffer trains
off the bridges And the birdies off
the telegraph wires .
That would never do would it for
the birds might get knocked off
and drowned? _ ducks don't often
perch on telegraph wires else it would be
all right. We have done as we were told.
   I didn't even say as some little
girls I know do. "I don't want."
No more news until I see you
tomorrow night .

                Your wandering Daddy
                    Come back.

FROM THE IRISH FREE STATE

Irish Free State

August 1923.

My dear Molly and Elizabeth.

    I was sorry I had to go
away again so soon this time in
a little ship. especially now that
Baby sister Ann has come to live
with us.

    I hope she is liking you both
for I know she and mummy are
very good chums and I want you
to like her too.

    It's quite strange how she came
to live with us for she wasn't
in the house when you both went
to bed the other night, and very
early in the morning she wasn't
about for I went to the doctorman's
house just as it was getting light.

    There were a lot of chirpy birds
about I noticed.

I knocked the doctor's door knocker
which had a lion's face and a
sleepy headed doctorman looked out
of his bed room window and asked
me "What was the matter?
I told him I thought there was a
baby coming to our house. He said
he had been up all night with a
case but would be along in a
minute.   Then he shut the window
with a bang!
It seemed to me like a BIG MINUTE
for it was quite light when he came
out. He came back with me and
went straight to mummy's room
and sure enough we heard a little
squeaky voice coming from the cot
beside mummy's bed, and there was
Baby Ann, quite happy as if she
was already used to living with us.
    The doctorman & Daddy were
just as surprised as you were when
you woke up & found you had a
Baby sister.

The doctorman told mummy she
could have a drink of tea and a bit
of toast, but Baby only got a
drink of water in a spoon which
seems an awful poor brecky
to go out into the world on.

Ireland is a funny country.
nearly as funny as Mexico.
I've been looking for a red pillar
box but only found one by chance
up a pudding bag lane that the
postman had forgotten to paint.

All the letter boxes are green
and the post offices too; the postmen's
coats are edged with it and on
their hats they wear a harp.
The Irish men seem very fond of
green. It cost two whole pennies
to send you a letter and with it
you get a green stamp with a
map of Ireland on it.

I was in such a funny
groceryman's to day, it wasn't

a bit like the ones at home.

The shop smelt so funny, of everything that ever went into a shop all mixed up together, an appley, bacony, beery sort of smell flavoured with kippers and yeast, and just a whiff of tar. The man who keeps this emporium calls himself not an Irish Grocerman but an _Italian Warehouseman_. He sells nearly everything. In one dark corner he sold drinks to big farmers who had come to market to sell their pigs + cows + butter. and in another was a large ticket which said

SHIPPING SUPPLIED

The shop was in a "muggle" as Liz says, and would have taken weeks and weeks to tidy up and get everything "Ship shape and Bristol fashion".

There were two or three big barrels
by the counter, and what do you
think was in them?
Salted pig's heads! big piggies,
little piggies, some with whiskers
and some quite bald.
I asked the grocery lady "If they were
from America" for which she did
not like me a bit, and said
"Indeed they were Irish pig's heads".
"And very cheap too"
I shall have to buy an Irish piggies
head for my dinner before I leave;
Of course the cook would have to soak
it a long time to get the salt out of it
and boil it for hours & hours to make
it tender.

Look after mother & Baby sister
Ann for me & see that mother has
nice flowers in her bed room
so be sure to pick them with great
long stems.

Cheery. O.
    All my love.
        Ever Your own Daddy

Irish Free State.
September 1923.

My dear Molly, Elizabeth & Ann.

Ireland is very beautiful specially in the autumn when all the creepers and trees are painted in such beutiful colours.

It is almost like an Indian Summer here but I miss the blue skies of Tampico but there is a lot to make up for it. The cathedral bells here play a ding-dong tune every afternoon at 4 o'clock, and they sound very beautiful on a still afternoon when the smoke from the little houses goes straight up into the sky.

The river is very winding and lovely and very deep at Passage. and Carrigaloe. The trees that fringe the side are nearly all evergreens, but where there is an autumn coloured tree its image

85

is reflected in the water and almost seems to set it on fire.

The people should be very happy here for the River Lee is much prettier than the Tamesi, but I miss the oil barges and the "Helen White", the stern wheeler that Beth wanted to cross the Atlantic in.

Today a fisherman in his little sailing boat asked me to give him a tow up to Cork so he could get his fishes to market while they were fresh and alive 0.

So I stopped my little boat & he has given me his line.

We are both going up quite fast with the tide and I hope he will get a lot of pennies for his fishes, for he has been sailing all night out with the sea-gulls which are dull company, and I know his little boys and girls must be hungry and waiting for their Daddy.

The river gets very narrow now
and the little boys & girls are all
out of school. They are standing on
the bank waving to us as we go
past. They have put their satchels
and books on the wall.
we wave back to them, for really it
is a friendly old world after all
I expect to sail soon for the West.

      Kiss mummy & Baby Ann for
me.

          Ever your Daddy.

P.S. The fisherman brought me a
     duck for myself as he got to
     market before the other fisherman
     sold his fish & got home early.

     I wish you could help me eat
     this duck & that someone else
     would give me some green peas
     to go with it.

Crookhaven.
October, 1923.

My dear Molly, 'Beth and Ann
    I sailed away last night but
the waves were very rough and my
little steam-boat got tossed about
like a cork.
I got down as far as the Fasnet
Lighthouse, a very high light-house
stuck on a little rock.
The waves and rain were driving
past it and the light only glowed
faintly like a halo that you see
round angels heads on glass
windows in churches.
The hand on the weather clock
was very low, and the old
man was out of the little cottage
so I thought the wind was going
to blow very hard. Big ships
they venture far, but little boats
stay by the shore so as I was

89

in a little boat. I just popped into
a little bay called Crookhaven
and let go the Anchor.

Nobody ever seems to go into
Crookhaven except little ships
like Daddy's when they are in
trouble and want shelter, that's
why they call it a haven!

It's got such a nice muddy
bottom so that if you should
lose your anchor it's all right;
no big holes will get knocked
into the ship by hard rocks.
You just sit nice and comfy
on the mud.

The waves were very high
And it was just getting light
as we passed the entrance to the haven
where there is a red light on one side
and a beacon (that is a pole with
a top mark) on the other.

The ship went up and down
& this way & then that, and it was

just like being on a switchback.

When we got inside we were ever so tired so all went fast asleep.

It was late afternoon when I awoke, so then I went ashore to the post office to shd word to mummy that I was sheltering out of the wind. I thought perhaps she would hear the windows rattling & be anxious.

A little old man wanted to change me a bag of potatoes for a bag of coal. You see there isn't any coal around here and the people burn turf. They have got loads of potatoes though. To change one thing that you have for something else you want is called TRADE by big grown up folks.

I went into a shop where they sold every thing. There was a girl there called Nellie and she wanted to sell me some home spun cloth

So I asked to see it for I thought
it would make mummy a good
costume?
I didn't know quite how much
to take so she asked how big mummy
was round the waist?.
That I couldn't tell her so to make
sure she told me to take another
yard as she was sure it would
not go to waste.
I Think she would have sold
Mr Selfridge lots, but very few
people come to buy at her little shop.

Love to all .
Ever your Daddy.

The light only glowed
faintly like a halo.

The old man was out
of his cottage.

Just like being on
a switch back.

Glengariff

November 1923.

My dear Molly Elizabeth & Ann.

Coming up Bantry Bay I met
a trawlerman; I said to him
"Good-morning Mr Fisherman
Give us a "fry" please"!
He gave us such a nice lot of fish
so we had them for "brecky" all
nice and tasty & fresh from the sea.

Glengariff is a very pretty
place, but ships dont often come
here, and then only little ones.
The bay is dotted with islands,
not cockatoo islands and alligator
cays like you see going to Mexico,
but rocky little islets with fairy
keeps and castles and towers where
giants lived long ago.

I kept a sharp look out for
princesses and princes who
might be in trouble, or held

Captive by the giants but I didn't
see any.
The woods at the back look very
gloomy and dark, and I think
dragons must have lived there long
ago, or did they stay right up on
the top of Hungry Hill, among the
caves of the bare looking mountain
in the distance with its peak wrapped
round with rain clouds?

I hardly knew my way into
the pier, and had to look often at
the chart which is a sailorman's
map. Have you noticed how
clever mummy is at finding her
way about strange places?
She has a sense of direction like
pigeons have which she calls
a "Bump of Locality".
I haven't much myself and have
to look often at the chart, and
sometimes when I can't see land
find where I am by the sun &
the stars.

I like the north star best because he
is easy to find and there are no
big sums to do when nce you've got him.
It's getting late here, but the hedges
are still made of fushia flowers
& the last of the blackberries are
still on the brambles.

Condensed milk is very dear
though, because the grocery man
never sells any except to an odd
sailorman or two who doesn't
want fresh cow's milk as it goes
sour if you keep it.

The water is beautiful and clear
here and you can see the bottom
and the fishes swimming about.
On the piles of the pier are very fine
muscles in blue & black shells.
We got a big net and gathered
two bucket fulls.

We should not have done so
if the shells had been clinging
to iron or copper, as perhaps they

97

would have made us bad.

He shall boil them in a pot
over a fire and eat them with
bread and butter for tea.
Under the rocks we found a lot
of winkles so we put them in
the pot "tambrin".
We had to get the winkles out of their
shells with a pin.
This should be a splendid place
to catch Red lobsters & crabs, which
are really black when they are alive
and go red when they are boiled.
They are caught in pots like this
which are anchored on the bottom,
The lobster goes in to get some bones
and can't find his way out again
& so gets caught!
Fish out of shells again for tea!
This has surely been a fishy
day!
They say that far away
fields are always greenest

98

if this could be possible in
this green little island.
any way when I get back I
think Daddy will go and look
for a "deep water" ship again
so I wouldn't be a bit surprised
if you get your next letter
from "any where"

Ever your own
Daddy.

The lobster
goes in here
→

FROM THE UNITED STATES OF AMERICA

S. S. "Minnie de Larrinaga"
Key West Channel.
4th January 1924

My dear Elizabeth.

Good-day Liz-gog how are you?
I am a very long way across the
water nearly as far as Mexico is.
We have been trying to race the sun
but he is still ahead of us and
we can't catch him up.
I expect that if we could we would
find he is setting in the hills
just behind Mrs Dodd's house
in Tampico.
We are going into port tomorrow
evening to a little place called
"Boco Grande" which means Big
Mouth where we are going to load
stuff to make all the flowers
and wheat grow nicely in the
fields at home. It is really the
bones of animals that lived years
ryears ago and is very good for the
ground.

What do you think? we have two
cats here. They are tabbies and
exactly like young tigers.
We are very fond of them both; one
we call Minnie and the other
her brother we Domingo.
During the day they find cosy
corners to have a nap in but at
night they creep stealthily about
looking for rats and mice.
Domingo likes rats best but
minnie prefers mice.
Sometimes minnie gets tired
of hunting big game and comes
up on to the bridge and helps
keep a look-out, for she can
like most cats see very well
in the dark.
She trots up and down rubbing
herself against your legs &
purrs in fine style.
When she gets tired of this she
goes into the chart-room and

lies full length upon the Chart.
and goes to sleep there.
She is a very forward cat indeed
I too am looking forward very
much to seeing you, molly and
Baby sister Ann and our very
good pal mother when I come
home again.
I hope you have been a good girl
and very kind to everyone.
Goodbye just now dear, I send
many kisses and a picture
of Minnie and Domingo;
their father was Felix the Cat.

FELIX

MIN

Domingo

Daddy.

S.S. "Minnie de Larrinaga"
Key West Channel.
7th January.24.

my dear molly,

Just a line to let you know that
I haven't got lost although we have
come a long way.
We shall be glad to get into port
tomorrow night for we are all tired
of rolling and tumbling about,
and as the ship has no cargo in
her she is light as a cork and
tossed to and fro by the waves.
I have been a little lonely without
you all, and I expect another has
too, so I hope you have been very
kind to her and given her an
unexpected kiss now and again
We had our Christmas at sea, but
cook made us a very good dinner
and we had turkey.
We missed of course all the

games and songs you have at home
and parties too.
How many parties did you go to
this year? I just love parties!
On Christmas day we played the
gramaphone on the hatch and had
a dance, but we were all men.
I think parties are best when there
is an equal number of boys and
girls. Don't you?
On a starry night can you tell
the difference between a star and
a planet?
A planet is a star that wanders about;
it is easy to tell them from the
stars as a star shines with a twinkling
light while a planet burns steadily
like the gas.
I saw a funny thing the other night
I looked through the glasses at a
big twinkling star and just
tapped the glasses with my finger
What do you think I saw?

All the twinkles spread out so that
it looked like a necklace made
of brilliants, rubies and emeralds,
the very choicest of stones.
Just the sort we would like to buy
mother if we were rich.
You ask mother to let you try one
night but you have to choose a
star with plenty of twinkle
in it.
Have you had any snow yet?
Isn't it strange to wake up in
the morning to find it a great
white world with only the footprints
of Mr Postman in the snow and
the birdies nearly buried up to
their wings.
Coming through "The Hole in
the Wall we saw coco-nut
palms growing
        They seemed to tell us that
although the skies are dull and
early we have to light up.

Spring won't be long coming. And
then "flying fish weather".
I have no more to tell you just
now dear.
I have written Elizabeth a letter
& told her about our cats, but I
haven't written to Ann for she
can't read yet can she?
By the way I found something
about the quiet way which
butterflies have in a paper
and I thought perhaps you would
like to learn it.
It is called "BUTTERFLY TOWN" but
it could easily have been called
"Under the old wall at Mayfield"
Here it is.

"Any bright day on the heathy down
You may hear the music of
Butterfly town"
"'Tis not very loud and not very strong"
"Just a murmurous hum, but an
old old song."
"Older than you or I   or Dad"
"Older than Grandfather when quite a lad.
"To the Roman who wandered long ago"
"In this same corner it still was so

This is very very important!
"The song they sing, only they can
hear who have a sympathetic ear.
"For even the wild bees underdrone
Roar like thunder above their own."
"And the breeze that sighs in the Alder
Copse
and bows altogether the nettle tops."
"Carries away with the thistle down
Those elfin strains of Butterflytown"

111

That's an easy two verses to learn
isn't it?
Goodnight just now dear   I shall
be delighted to see you when I
get back.

Best love from Daddy.

S.S. "Minnie de Larrinaga"
Galveston
Texas.
(Where the cotton grows).
16th January 1924

My dear Molly and Elizabeth
Just a line to tell you that
I received dear mothers letter
this morning and she told me you
were all very well.
We are now at Galveston waiting
to load cotton. It grows here
on a low bush, and black men
gather it and press it into big
bundles and then load it down
the big hold of the ship.
We bring it all the way to
Manchester where they take it
from us and spin it into thread
so that mother can sew with it.
We do not bring wool what
mummy darns our socks with

for that comes from the fleece of
the sheep. There are no sheep here
however.
What do you think?
As we came along far out at sea
a pelican bird settled on the foremast
and stayed there all day
When he saw the land he flapped
his big wings and flew away to
the shore.
He lives in the low marshes by
the sea-coast and eats for his
dinner fishes.
He hovers around high up in the air
and when he sees a fish in the
water he drops down like a stone
and swallows the fish whole.
He has a tremendous big beak,
it holds quite nine pints I think
that's heaps of jug fulls like
Aunt Mary puts in the coffee.

Our two cats. "Minnie" and
"Domingo" are well
Domingo is in disgrace as he
went down the dirty bunkers
and got his fur all very black.
He ought to have licked himself
clean but no, he was lazy
and crept up to the wireless
man's cabin and went to sleep
on his ~~only~~ only clean shirt, making
it black as black can be.
In the "Minnie" we only like
clean and careful pussies!
Do you still play at shops?
I wonder if you have ever heard
of "The Fairy Market" it's all
about the fairies playing with
the flowers.

"Fairies! Buy our dainty goods"
"Here are velvet pansy hoods"
"Bows & bonnets, frocks and frills"
"Culled from Golden daffodils"
"Filmy stuffs of thistle down"
"Fit to make a summer gown"
"Seek our market in the woods"
"Fairies buy our dainty goods"

—

"Fairies! buy our dainty goods"
"Leafy aprons, cobweb snoods"
"dew drop pearls to trim a frock"
"Come & buy our pretty stock"
"Gossamer the spiders spun"
"Hats to shield you from the sun"
"Seek our market in the woods"
"Fairies buy our dainty goods!"

Give mother & little Ann kisses
from me & I send some to
yourselves
                    Daddy.

X X X X X X X X X X X

Golden Daffodils

"Gossamer the spiders spun

Piscado

say Cap
I'm not a
steple jack

Ratones

Minnie turns her
back on James
the Pelican

* Piscado = fish

* Ratones = mice

S.S. Minnie de Larrinaga
Savannah.

St Valentine's Eve 1924

My dear Molly Elizabeth & Ann.

Just a line to tell you I am
looking forward to seeing you
all again at the beginning of
March. I hear you have been
having such a lot of snow.
Isn't it strange to wake up
in the morning and find how
busy Jack Frost has been
painting trees and ferns upon
the window pane. And then to
look down into 'the garden &
see a "white world"; the trees
all iced like a birthday cake?
Then there are the tracks of the
milkman and the Post man
and sometimes when you look

119

very closely on the lawn you
can find little marks like this

       γ   γ
      γ   γ
     γ   γ
    γ   γ

This is where a Robin Red breast
has been coming near to the
house to look for stray crumbs
The pussies leave marks like
this which are very different
to those of the birdies.

Yesterday I went to Church early
and what do you think I saw in
the square right in the middle of
the big City? a beautiful grey
squirrel with a bushy tail like this.

He was nibbling at a fir cone
and was quite tame.
He had his home in the hollow of a
tree near by, but isn't it strange
that he should live in the middle
of a big city when his proper home
is in the shady woods
I gave him a pea-nut but he did
not eat it but dug a little hole
with his fore paws and hid it
in the turf.
I expect he had enough dinner
for today, and put the nut
away for tomorrow when it

might be cold and snowy and
fir cones hard to find.
I just love squirrels don't you?
their coats are very silky that's
why they make such fine fur coats.
They are very fond of acorns when
they can get them; acorns are
the seed of the oak tree that is
so big & strong that it is used for
making ships. From them big
oak trees grow. would you like to
try to grow one all by your own
selves? You two little girls go out
into the woods and look for an
acorn amongst the dead leaves.
They are not hard to find.
Bring it home carefully, then ask
mummy for an orange with a
thick skin.
Get a spoon & eat all the juicey
inside out of it through a little
hole in the top.

You now fill up the orange that only has his skin left with sweet smelling loam you find under hedges and stick the acorn in the hole, right side up of course for it would never do to have him standing on his head.

Then you give it the weeniest drop of water every day and bye & bye you have a lovely little oak tree, that looks as if it had weathered so many stormy winters growing snugly in an orange.

No more news.

Ever your own Daddy

P.S.

I am wondering whether the crocuses are coming up in the garden yet.
Are they?

Liverpool
March 1924.

My dear Molly, Elizabeth & Ann.

Just a line to let you know that we have arrived back safely, and I hope to get a run home as soon as the stevadores get a little cargo out.

The ship brought a lot of turpentine in barrels; that's the stuff that the paintermen put in paint to make it dry quickly so that it does not get on little girls' clean pinnies. It runs out of the trunks of trees into little pots.

Black men loaded it into the ship. It is very hard work but they are very strong and big so don't mind.

They get paid their wages every night for the work they do.

125

And if any of them has been lazy
the "Big Boss" shouts out at the
end of the day.
"Goodbye Horace!"
"Goodbye Cedric"!
Then they know not to come looking
for work in the morning.
It seems quite a pleasant way.
This trip you nearly said Good-bye
Daddy! for the wind blew very
hard and the sea rose very high
and threatening black clouds came
rolling up from the South East.
It was a very dark dark night
at midnight when Cinderella
lost her slipper you will remember.
Heaps of green water was washing
around the decks; big lumps
that sailormen call "dollups"
came aboard and were getting
down the skylight in the bows
of her, so I went forward with
four sailors and a piece of canvas
to tie over it.

I had a flash light in my hand
and had only begun to get busy
when Bang a big wave came up
and hit Daddy such a smack.
The Captain said that the torch
went up to the lower mast head,
but I didn't know anything.
Wasn't it strange the big bang
put me right off to sleep?
When I woke up I was all wet
through and hanging with one leg
over the side below the bridge.
And with me were two other
sailormen MR. Bin Ali and
Mr Ali Bin Mahomed I never
knew their home address but
they lived in Bootle.

The captain picked us up and
carried us into his cabin where
he gave us something hot as
we were very cold with our teeth
chattering.

I only had a few cuts but the other
two had broken legs.
The captain was very kind, he
made a doctor's shop of the cabin
and tried to make us all better.
I was soon well and about again,
but the other two had to have their
legs tied up between pieces of wood
and plaster of paris : what they mend
cracks in ceilings with.
The both of them had to lie very
still; had jelly to eat and lots
of rice pudding but not much
meat.
When the ship got here they drove
away in a very fine ambulance
all white with a big Red Cross
on it. That's the mark that is
always on cars that take about
sick people.
         Soon the legs of Ali Bin
Mahomed and Bin Ali will
be mended again when they

128

will go and look for a ship.
and go down to the sea again
all merry & bright.
Good. bye just now I must
go away and move some
barrels of turps
I wish you three little girls were
here to help me.
You would be a help!

Ever your Daddy.

London
April 1924.

My dear ~~Molly~~ Elizabeth & Ann,

It really is fine to be back once
again on the coast for it really
is the best way to go to sea,
for instead of the deep blue water
there are the rivers and fields
left o o brown where the ploughs
have been.

The little towns, the drying creeks
the marshes so full of water at
high spring tides all are so ~~full
of interest~~ jolly.

I've just landed at "Dust Hole"
steps. The April evening sunlight
is making the houses and church
stand out, & touched the roofs
with gold so that it looks like
a fairy scene.

A crowd of little girls and boys
have come down & want to look
after the boat. I gave them a penny
and the biggest girl wants to know
"How far this is going between them"?
I told her to buy some acid drops
and share them out.
I'm very glad it is not raining, for
then every one seems so grumpy
and growly to each other.
You soon will be going to school
and learn geography. Teacher
will make you learn the names of
the rivers Daddy goes up, and
the heights of the different mountains,
but you better start by learning
this old rhyme which even perhaps
teacher doesn't know.

"When it's high water at London Bridge
"It's half ebb in the Swin."
"Low water in Yarmouth Roads"
"But half flood at Lynn"

"First the Dudgeon"
        "Then the Spurn"
"Flamboro' Head comes next in turn"
"Twice white once red" , ""
        "That's the light on Flamboro' Head.
"Scarboro' Castle stands at sea".
    "Whitby Rocks bear NORTHERLY."
    "Huntcliff Foot with its high backed
                                    land"
"   Twenty Seven miles from Sunderland"
"   Sunderland stands in the BIGHT"
        "Just nine miles from Tynemouth ,,
                            Light."

Still you can't have every thing,
for if you have the little towns
and lights and boys you can't have
the deep blue rolling sea & the great cliffs
It has to be either one or the other!
I listened in Church to a story
the other day.
It was about a quaint old man
who went about selling worms.

133

He used to go in front of his
gaily painted cart shouting
"A worm for a feather"
      "A worm for a feather".
A young skylark heard him
and commenced to give the little
old man one of his tail feathers
in exchange for a fat juicy worm.
At first he didn't miss his
feathers for it was so easy to
get worms that way
But after a while the sky lark
found he could not go as far as
he used to do ~ fly as high as
of old.
This began to worry him, so one
day he saw he had made a
mistake by getting his worms
"the easy way". so he got up
very early and gathered a
big basket right full up.
      He took them to the little
old man and told him he
                    would

give him all the big basket of
worms if only he would give
him his feathers back.
But the old man old laughed
& said.
"Worms for feathers is my trade,
         not feathers for worms "Sonny".

The poor little skylark died.

Now that I'm coasting I may
not be able to write any more
long letters for it is "Up and
under all the time".
All the rest of my letters you
may forget but always remember
the story of the skylark.
It may help you sometime.

                    Ever your loving
                         Daddy.

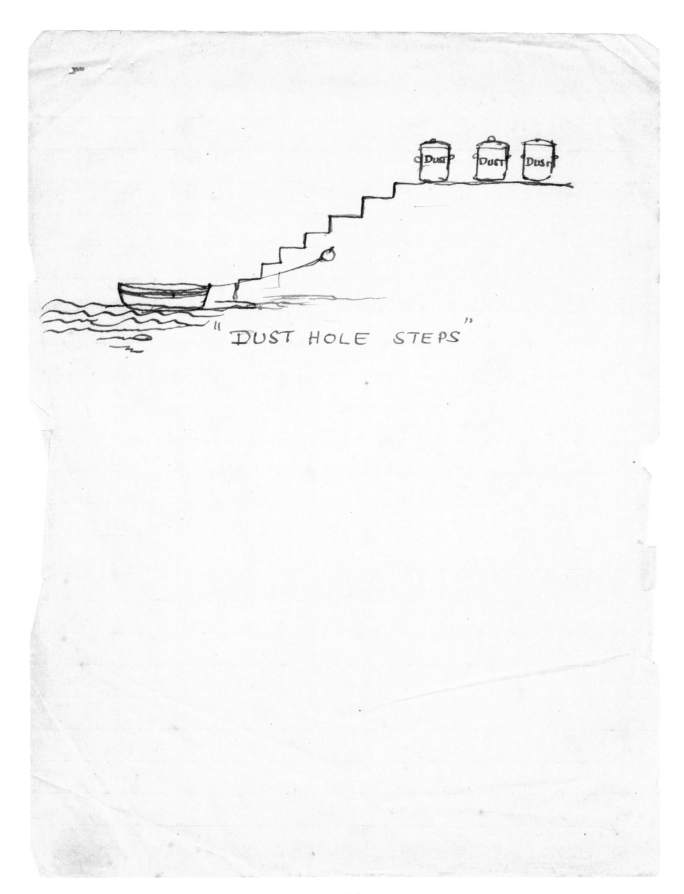

"DUST HOLE STEPS"

AFTERWORD

The Port of London Authority again employed Arthur John Booth in 1925, this time dredging the corners of East India and Norway docks, and on completion the PLA put general dredging to contract. Shipping was in decline worldwide and he began to search for a new job.

He applied to the Colonial Office and was offered an appointment with the Kenya Uganda Railways & Harbours Company. He sailed on the Union Castle *SS Gascon* to Mombasa and served the KUR&H from 1925 to 1946. He was Second Mate, First Mate and then Commander on the ships sailing on Lake Victoria and Lake Albert. He also sailed up the Kagera River, which he always believed to be the source of the River Nile in the Ruwenzori Mountains.

During this time, his wife sailed five times by liner to spend a year, mid-contract, in Africa living both in Kisumu, Kenya and Butiaba in Uganda. The children were in boarding school when she was abroad and spent holidays with relatives in Scotland and Yorkshire. In 1935 Molly accompanied her mother travelling via South Africa to Mombasa, returning via the Suez Canal. In 1938 Elizabeth enjoyed a similar "round" trip arriving back with her mother only days before the Second World War broke out in September 1939.

In the final years of the war, Mary Booth was able to rejoin Arthur Booth in Kenya until his retirement in late 1946, when they sailed in the *Winchester Castle* for England and onwards to their home in Yorkshire. Arthur Booth joined the Sea Cadet Corps in Leeds in March 1948 and when they moved to Deganwy in North Wales early in the 1950s, he was transferred to the Llandudno & District Sea Cadets until he retired from the Corps in 1962. In Deganwy, he spent a couple of years as Harbour Master at Conway and then applied as summer relief on the London County Council sewage ships on the Thames - the "Bovril" boats based at Beckton.

His final years were spent in Portishead near his daughter Elizabeth where he built a house overlooking the Severn Estuary. The telescope was always in the window to watch the ships sailing to and from the ports. As is shown in his letters to his children, he always enjoyed sketching and illustration and he now had time to write his memoirs and paint. Sometimes he painted on canvas, but he also used corrugated cardboard, wood and the lids of tea chests. The wealth of paintings from this period depict his lifelong adventure at sea and serve as a powerful visual accompaniment to his memoirs.

Running the easting down – AJ Booth. Oil on board 47cm x 31cm

For many years Arthur Booth was Honorary Treasurer of the Bristol Shiplovers' Society, which met monthly in the Sailors' Home in Bristol. Arthur and Mary celebrated their Diamond Wedding in 1977 and Arthur died on his 89th birthday in 1980. Mary died on her 100th birthday in 1989. In his will, Arthur's last words were - "and in salute my Red Ensign lowers gently down".

MARIDADI PUBLISHING